Original title:
The Orchard's Bounty

Copyright © 2025 Creative Arts Management OÜ
All rights reserved.

Author: Vivian Laurent
ISBN HARDBACK: 978-1-80586-257-4
ISBN PAPERBACK: 978-1-80586-729-6

Embrace of the Earth's Generosity

In the garden, apples wear hats,
Peaches dance like carefree cats.
Tomatoes gossip in the sun,
Cucumbers plotting pranks for fun.

Cherries giggle, red and round,
While lemons burst out with a sound.
Radishes playing hide and seek,
Mocking the turnips, oh so meek.

Quintessence of Life and Light

Carrots dreaming of high-speed chases,
Potatoes striking silly poses.
Zucchinis with their long, green flair,
Bask in sunshine without a care.

The beets wear boots, so very bright,
Salsa dancers in the night.
Garlic grows with style and grace,
Whispering secrets to the space.

Berry Breezes and Lemon Whispers

Blueberries in a merry parade,
Raspberries have a masquerade.
Strawberries plan a weekend trip,
With ice cream cones, they start to skip.

Lemons sardine like a troupe,
In their yellow, zesty loop.
Peas pop jokes, all in a row,
Their laughter spreads, a vibrant glow.

Fertile Dreams of Springtime

In spring's embrace, the veggies grin,
With every sprout, they twist and spin.
Onions tell tales, a bit too sour,
While radishes boast of their power.

Cabbages wear crowns made of leaves,
While pumpkins plot on rolling eves.
In this land where glee is sown,
Nature's joy is truly grown.

Fruiting Bonds of Earth and Sky

In the garden, apples roll,
Chasing shadows, on a stroll.
Lemons whisper, just for fun,
Hey there, friend! Let's bask in sun.

Grapes compose a merry tent,
Offering shade, they're heaven-sent.
Cherries giggle, flip and flop,
Making every pickle stop!

Breath of Life in Each Harvest

Peaches plop into the basket,
Each one stutters, 'I can't last it!'
Lettuce laughs in leafy chance,
Twirling, dancing in a trance.

Tomatoes blush like cheeky teens,
Whispering tales of salad dreams.
Zucchini sings a silly tune,
Telling jokes beneath the moon.

Life Unfurled Among the Leaves

Mangoes hide in branches high,
Joking with the breezy sky.
Avocado, smooth and sleek,
Shares its wisdom, 'Just be chic!'

Oranges juggling in a vine,
Trading secrets, oh how fine!
RSS says, 'Let's spread the cheer!'
Life's too short; just grab a pear!

A Song of Trees and Time

Willows sway and sing a tune,
Tickling squirrels with a swoon.
Pines propose a dance tonight,
Under stars, they spin with light.

Cacti crack the best of jokes,
While teasing all the thirsty folks.
Peppers start a spicy brawl,
Yet somehow, they all stand tall!

Shadows Cast by Golden Apples

Golden apples dangle high,
With shadows that dance, oh my!
A squirrel in a turtleneck,
Claims each fruit with grand respect.

The wind plays tricks, a cheeky breeze,
Sending leaves swirling with such ease.
A raccoon winks from the tree's embrace,
Stealing bites with a mischievous grace.

Savoring the Seasons

Spring comes in with a blossom giggle,
While bees buzz past with a jolly wiggle.
Summer's heat brings a juicy grin,
As watermelons roll in a bright spin.

Fall chuckles with leaves that twirl,
While pumpkins chase the wind in a whirl.
Winter's chill wraps tight like a hug,
As apples snicker on a frosty rug.

The Language of Leaves and Seeds

Leaves whisper secrets in the breeze,
While seeds giggle, hiding with ease.
Roots plot mischief deep in the ground,
As nature's laughter echoes around.

A sunflower bows with a shy delight,
While night critters dance till the morning light.
Each rustle and shuffle, a joyous sound,
In the garden's chat, friendships abound.

Treasures from the Fertile Ground

Digging deep, what will I find?
A dancing carrot, smart and aligned.
Potatoes chuckle as they're pulled from the mud,
Sharing stories of their earthy blood.

With each harvest, a funny surprise,
Tomatoes blush and onions disguise.
While beetroot wears its best party face,
Nature's treasures, a jovial embrace.

Ripe Memories in the Breeze

A fruit flew by with a giggle,
It made me laugh, even made me wiggle.
A pear told jokes, a peach laughed loud,
Together they formed a juicy crowd.

The grapes had a party, quite the scene,
Dancing on vines, all dressed in green.
Bananas slipped, oh what a mess!
Even apples joined, in their Sunday best!

Orchard Dreams at Dusk

When twilight fell, the cherries conspired,
To send out raccoons, quite inspired.
They gathered the nuts, playing a prank,
While squirrels chased shadows, their ships set to sank.

The moon smiled down on the fruit brigade,
As lemons rolled dice, their fortune to trade.
With laughter and zest, they danced in delight,
While peaches sang songs under soft twilight.

Secrets of the Fertile Ground

The soil whispered tales of splendor,
Of tomatoes wearing hats of great gender.
Radishes blushed, embarrassed yet proud,
While carrots cheered softly, lost in the crowd.

The roots held secrets, quite the delight,
Of midnight feasts under twinkling light.
A turnip recited a tale of the past,
Of days gone by, and fun unsurpassed!

Bounty Beneath the Boughs

Beneath the branches, shenanigans grew,
With peppers that tangoed, won daringly too.
Cucumbers giggled, with crickets in tune,
As sunflowers swayed like a comical typhoon.

A watermelon statue was built with finesse,
But it rolled away, oh what a mess!
The laughter erupted, joyous and bright,
In a carnival of chaos, pure delight.

Fruits of Nature's Embrace

Apples rolling down the lane,
Chasing squirrels, what a game!
Peaches giggle, ripe and sweet,
Oranges bounce upon their feet.

Bananas slip, oh what a sight,
Lemons squirt in sheer delight!
Fruits in hats, they dance around,
Laughter echoes, joy is found.

Whispers of the Harvest Moon

Under moonlight, fruits unite,
Grapes in pajamas, quite the sight!
Avocados having tea, so grand,
While melons play in a rock band.

Cider flows like bubbly streams,
Carrots tease, 'We are the dreams!'
Twinkling stars in the night's embrace,
Fruits in frolic, a playful race.

Secrets Beneath the Branches

Beneath the trees, a party brews,
Berries gossip, sharing news.
Pears in line for the latest trend,
Cherries whisper, 'We must blend!'

Nuts are juggling, not a care,
Figs are posing, debonair.
With twinkling eyes and silly hats,
Nature giggles, imagine that!

Echoes of Autumn's Lullaby

Leaves are rustling, fruits asleep,
Pumpkins giggle, secrets keep.
Squashes sing their low, deep tune,
While spices dance beneath the moon.

Jars of jam on shelves so wide,
Pickles waltz with fussy pride.
In the cool air, laughter swells,
Nature's jokes, oh how it tells!

Nectar of the Earth's Generosity

In the garden, apples grin,
Waving at the neighbors' kin.
Peaches flirting with the breeze,
Plums sneaking snacks behind the trees.

Ripe berries bounce from bush to bush,
Laughing as the squirrels rush.
Bananas slip with joyful squeaks,
Even carrots play hide-and-seek.

Grapes gossip on the vine,
Sipping sunlight like good wine.
Cherries burst, a berry fight,
Tickling tongues with sheer delight.

Lemons joke, a little sour,
Telling tales of sunny power.
Nature's bounty, bold and bright,
Sprinkles giggles, pure delight.

The Yearning of Fruitful Hearts

Mangoes dream of tropical seas,
Dancing down with sticky knees.
Oranges juggle, bold and round,
In this crazy fruit playground.

Peppers prank the timid squash,
Whispering tales of a garden posh.
Zucchini zips with green delight,
Chasing butterflies in flight.

Corn on the cob makes silly faces,
Popping jokes in crowded spaces.
Radishes play the stealthy game,
Hiding from the salad's fame.

Tomatoes blush when they're called out,
On pizza nights, they twist and shout.
In this crammed and fruity cheer,
Everyone's welcome, bring your beer!

A Portrait of Nature's Generosity

A pumpkin wore a funny hat,
Wishing it were more than that.
A scarecrow nods, a foe's delight,
Waving at the moonlit night.

Berry bushes sway and sway,
Chasing bumblebees all day.
Cucumbers prank the old oak tree,
Telling tales of jubilee.

Eggplants quest for stylish flair,
Trying hard to dress with care.
Peas in pods are quite the gang,
Bursting forth with every clang.

Fruits and veggies gather 'round,
Sharing laughs without a sound.
In this portrait, bold and bright,
Nature's giggles take to flight.

The Melodies of Harvest Time

Harvest moon, a disco ball,
Fruits parade, they give their all.
Veggies croon a silly song,
In this festival, they all belong.

Baskets rolling through the lanes,
Dancing past the silly trains.
Bananas swing on crooked vines,
Making up their own punchlines.

Carrots tap their leafy feet,
Grooving to a funky beat.
Radishes spin with wild glee,
Twirling round for all to see.

With every laugh, a crop is born,
As twilight whispers, 'Don't be worn.'
The melodies of joyful cheer,
Fill the fields as harvest draws near.

Harvest Moon Serenade

Under the moon, the apples dance,
A squirrel wore pants, took a chance.
He twirled with glee, oh what a sight,
While owls watched on, laughing with fright.

Pumpkins roll by, with a jig and a cheer,
They sang quite loud, 'It's harvest year!'
The scarecrows clapped, made of hay,
As bunnies joined in, hip-hip-hooray!

Sweetness in the Sunlight

Peaches are blushing beneath a bright sun,
While bees in tuxedos just buzz and run.
Marmalade dreams drip from tree limbs,
Sipping the nectar, oh how it brims!

The berries giggle, their laughter so sweet,
As ants in top hats come out for a treat.
Cherries play tag with raccoons in flight,
'You can't catch me!' they scream with delight.

Nature's Cornucopia Unveiled

Carrots wear shades, they soak in the warmth,
While radishes rise, all proud of their charm.
Tomatoes are rolling, they slip and they slide,
With cucumbers cracking up, unable to hide!

Eggplants play poker, so suave and so sleek,
While lettuce declares, 'I'm fab and unique!'
A corn stalk shimmies, a dance with a twist,
'Oh veggie friends, we cannot be missed!'

Blossoms Beneath the Clouds

Daisies are gossiping, all in a flurry,
While bees wear fedora, they're always in a hurry.
Tulips break dance, on the whimsical breeze,
While grass blades gossip, oh do they tease!

The sunflowers wave, with a wink and a grin,
As crickets on violins play a cheeky din.
With petals in uproar, and laughter so loud,
Springing new mischief, beneath the soft cloud.

Dawn of the Fruitful Harvest

Sunrise peeks through leafy greens,
Energetic squirrels plan their scenes.
One jumps high with a nut in toe,
While the others argue, 'You're too slow!'

The pumpkins roll down, a comical sight,
While birds chirp laughs, taking flight.
A dance of colors paints the ground,
As laughter echoes all around.

A Dance with the Mellow Wind

Wind whispers sweet nothings, quite absurd,
Tickling the apples, so soft, unheard.
A pear does a twist and a little jig,
While cherries cheer, bouncing on a twig.

Squirrels mime dance moves, hip and funky,
They trip on acorns, oh how clunky!
The branches sway, join the delight,
In fruit-filled frolic, from morning to night.

Fruits of Autumn's Embrace

Oranges plump, they plot a scene,
To roll down the hill, all bright and keen.
But one gets stuck—what a melodrama!
His pals just laugh, 'Oh, fruit-a-rama!'

Beneath a tree, the berries gossip,
"Did you see that? He's lost his grip!"
With autumn's humor in the breeze,
They sway and giggle behind the leaves.

Whispers of Glistening Leaves

Leaves rustle secrets, giggles in the sun,
As twirling fruits have their playful fun.
A grape rolls past with a cheeky grin,
While friendly nuts join in on the spin.

Laughter bubbles up from the ground,
As the juicy crew serenades the sound.
A harvest parade, all colors bold,
With funny tales of treasures untold.

Abundance in the Canopy

Up in the trees, fruits are swinging,
Squirrels mumble, their teeth are clinging,
A pear drops down with a plop and a thud,
My hat's now a bowl—what a juicy flood!

Lemonade rain falls from yellowed skies,
I catch a grapefruit, oh what a surprise!
The apples are laughing, their cheeks flush with mirth,
I'm wondering if this is a fruit-giving birth.

Sunlit Pathways of Delight

Strolling through rows where shadows dance,
Strawberries winking in summer's romance,
Cherries are giggling, a bold little bunch,
They roll off the branches, oh, what a punch!

Lemon trees whisper sweet citrus schemes,
As I dodge tangerines bursting at seams,
An orange thuds down, it's quite a sight,
Only in fruit land are fights so polite.

Scented Petals and Tender Roots

Petals are waving like hands on a spree,
Bees buzzing choruses, oh, what a key!
The tulips boast colors that wiggle with flair,
While daisies seek gossip in thickets of air.

Roots underground strike a deal with worms,
Their secret plans lead to fruity firms,
If veggies could giggle, they'd roar with savings,
"Carrots for cash? Oh, the fruit market's cravings!"

The Taste of Earth's Generosity

A basket of goodies, a colorful sight,
Peaches in a pillow, such a soft bite,
Banana peels slipping, a comedic glee,
Caught in the act—was it me or the tree?

Ripe figs and melons are bold in their games,
Making me wonder how fruit knows my names,
I stumble and tumble, it's all in good fun,
Sweet harvest laughs as I slip on a pun!

Ripened Joy on the Vine

Grapes in a brawl, they tumble and roll,
Poking each other, playing their role.
A juicy debate, who's sweeter, who's ripe?
Tasting their way through a grapevine hype.

One shouted, "I'm better! I'm bursting with charm!"
While another just giggled and swayed with alarm.
Together they laughed, in the sun's golden light,
Two silly old fruits, what a comical sight!

Sweet Whispers Among the Branches

Peaches were gossiping, oh what a scene,
Discussing the weather and who wore what green.
One flaunted its fuzz and the other its glow,
"Mine's the best dress!" said the queen of the show.

As they argued, a berry joined in with a song,
"Stop all this chatter! You're just stringing it wrong!"
But laughter erupted, a sweet frolicsome cheer,
For joyful convos brought them all near.

Golden Moments in Every Bite

An apple and pear sat under the tree,
Making a plan for a jolly spree.
They schemed to roll down to the picnic below,
Hoping to land in the jam—what a show!

"Oh, what a twist! We'll spread joy sublime!"
Squealed the apple, who fancied some crime.
"Just think of the giggles when we land in the bowl,
A fruity explosion; oh, what a goal!"

Journey to the Heart of Growth

Sprouts bursting forth, all ready to play,
"Come on, little buddies, let's grow into stray!"
They wiggled and jiggled, up through the dirt,
Each tiny vine laughing, no matter the hurt.

"Who'd ever thought that we'd make quite a scene,
In this glorious patch of a green, leafy dream?"
From budding to blossoming, they danced in delight,
Finding pure joy in their growth and their plight.

Fragrant Paths of Fruity Bliss

In a garden where apples giggle,
And pears wear hats to make you wiggle,
Bananas dance with a silly grin,
While cherries play tag, let the fun begin!

Peaches are plotting a merry prank,
As plums float by on a grapevine plank,
Lemons are laughing, a zesty crew,
With limes that wink and say, "We've got juice too!"

Ripe berries burst with laughter bright,
While oranges juggle in pure delight,
The fruits parade in their colorful dress,
In this quirky patch, there's no time for stress!

So join the fun, grab your fruit hat,
Join dancing grapes, and don't sit flat,
In this realm where every bite's a tease,
Come taste the joy, oh, if you please!

Fluttering Wings and Blossoms

Butterflies sip from blossoms sweet,
While a bee buzzes with two left feet,
Daisies tickle the sparrow's toes,
As tulips whisper, 'Shh! Here comes the prose!'

Cherries think they're comedians bold,
Telling jokes that never get old,
While daisies giggle behind leafy screens,
At the antics of mischievous bean machines.

The tulips twirl, trying their best,
In a dance-off with a bold little pest,
In a world where pollen's the currency fun,
There's laughter in each raindrop spun!

So flutter along, chase the blooms,
Join the laughter, dispel the glooms,
In this garden of joy, life's all a game,
With buzzing friends that bring you fame!

Synchrony of Fruit and Foliage

An apple juggles with a peach in tow,
While berries in bikinis steal the show,
Grapefruits roll on a lemon's back,
Creating a circus in a fruity shack!

Leaves are clapping as fruits perform,
To the rhythm of sunshine, they keep warm,
Kiwi and mango, a duet divine,
With giggles and wiggles, how they shine!

Bananas slip in a slapstick routine,
While figs play the role of the skeptical queen,
Oranges spin tales of sweet ambition,
In a land where fruit dreams find their mission!

Join this fiesta in the sun's soft glow,
Where every bite's a laughing bow,
In the trees where humor meets the vine,
Life's a fruity dance, oh how they shine!

Lyrical Offerings from the Earth

Raspberry rhymes weave tales in the air,
As cucumbers sigh in their leafy chair,
Lemons serenade with a zesty zest,
In a garden where laughter feels truly blessed!

Tomatoes roll with a giggling flair,
Waving their greens, without a care,
Peppers debate on the funniest line,
While squash makes puns that are truly fine!

Herbs join in with a jazzy beat,
Basil's beats make the whole crowd fleet,
Oregano's jokes might make you sneeze,
But parsley's charm will surely please!

So gather around for this lyrical spree,
Where vegetables bond like bumblebee,
In the earth's embrace, humor takes root,
Join this nature's show, feel the fruity loot!

Blossoms and Shadows of Time

Once I tripped on fallen pears,
My dance turned to a somersault,
The bees all buzzed, I waved in flair,
While chasing after ripe results!

Through tangled vines and splintered wood,
I found a stash of nuts and fruits,
With squirrels laughing, oh so good,
They knew my secret for cute suits!

The blossoms laughed at my bad luck,
They bloomed a little fierce and bright,
But still, the ground held playful muck,
A tasty trap of pure delight!

So here's a toast, with juice in hand,
To every stumble that we face,
In bouncing ballads of this land,
Where each mistake brings fruity grace!

The Dance of Orchard Spirits

In the moonlight, fruits take flight,
With cherries winking, grapes in tow,
A jig of plums, all dressed so bright,
They whirl and twirl, a fruity show!

Those sneaky spirits sip and sway,
With every sip of cider fair,
They bounce around the night and play,
Causing mischief everywhere!

An apple fell and bumped my nose,
I laughed at pears that rolled away,
As fig leaves danced, it surely shows,
That fun will always find a way!

So join the dance, get up, don't stay,
Embrace the laughter, swell with cheer,
In orchards where the spirits play,
We'll chase the fruits, our joy sincere!

A Symphony of Color and Taste

Bananas strum like golden strings,
With lemon zests that add the beat,
Each fruit a note that sweetly sings,
In harmony, we dance on feet!

Peaches blush and shimmy near,
While apples boast in shiny tones,
A melody that brings such cheer,
The fruit parade, it calls us home!

A raspberry shrieked, "I can't keep still!"
While blackberries rolled into a groove,
Together bursting with fruity thrill,
They made the whole garden move!

The jam I spilled became a tune,
A sticky rhythm on the beat,
We laughed until the night was noon,
In our sweet world of joy and heat!

Beneath the Canopy of Abundance

Beneath the leaves, a dappled show,
Tomatoes quipped with witty jests,
The cucumbers, their shoulder slow,
Turned veggies into silly pests!

A squash named Sam sang high and loud,
His melody made pumpkins grin,
While carrots hid beneath the crowd,
Afraid of being pulled for sin!

The raindrops laughed upon the earth,
With every splash, a giggle grew,
Each fruit and veggie brought such mirth,
They played from dawn till evening's dew!

So here's our toast, beneath the trees,
To all the laughs that nature shares,
In every root, in every breeze,
Let joy abound—we have no cares!

Tales from the Lush Canopy

Once a pear danced with delight,
Wobbling left, then wobbled right.
A squirrel chuckled, 'What a sight!'
'Careful now, you'll take flight!'

The apple rolled upon the ground,
Complaining, 'Why am I so round?'
A pigeon cooed without a sound,
'You're the best snack to be found!'

Cherries squeaked, and peaches pranced,
While plums blushed in a merry dance.
They spun and twirled in a fruit-filled trance,
Declaring, 'Life is but a chance!'

When shadows grew and dusk was near,
Bananas yelled, 'Let's have some cheer!'
The laughter echoed far and clear,
As nature's joy brought us all near.

Reverie of Ripeness and Resilience

In a tree, a grapefruit grinned,
'Who knew this life would feel like wind?'
A breeze came in, and leaves rescind,
Saying, 'Chill out, don't offend!'

Peaches shared a silly tale,
Of a fruit who wished to sail.
'Just wait for rain, you'll hit the trail,'
They laughed till they began to pale.

A berry declared, 'I'm feeling bold,
With my hues of red and gold!'
'You've got a story yet untold,'
Whispered a fig, half-subtle, half old.

At sunset, fruits wore crowns of dusk,
Celebrating life with zest and musk.
While bugs played tunes, a lively fuss,
All together, without a bus.

Glistening Gems of Summer's End

Underneath the sun's warm gaze,
Berries twinkled in a daze.
'We're not just treats, we're also plays!'
The grapes chimed in, 'Let's start a craze!'

With a wink, the cherries swung,
'This party's ripe; let's get it sprung!'
Some apples chimed, 'We're still so young!'
Dancing till the night's bell rung.

Melons brought a juicy jest,
'Why are fruit flies always the guest?'
Peaches sighed, 'They love the best,
But we'll outshine all the rest!'

As twilight spread its gentle hue,
All fruits sang a happy tune.
Joyful memories by the moon,
Ready for more, they all attune.

Bountiful Heartbeats Under the Sky

A lemon squirted with a smile,
'I sour, but I sure have style!'
A lime replied, 'Just stay a while,
Together we can share our guile!'

On the branch, a kumquat bragged,
'Small but fierce, I'm never ragged.'
The others cheered, no one was lagged,
'Let's make a feast before we're snagged!'

As night fell, stars gleamed like spices,
Fruits discussed their dreams and vices.
'Let's clash our colors, no more slices!'
They painted skies with their devices.

And so beneath the moonlit dome,
Fruits found laughter, love, and home.
Connected by the space we roam,
In every heart, there lies a poem.

Echoes of the Harvest

In the fields where apples grow,
The trees whisper tales, you know.
A squirrel dances, doing its jig,
While bees buzz round with a giggly dig.

Pumpkins roll, they round and stout,
Chasing each other, make a route.
The scarecrow winks, he's seen it all,
And laughs with crows at their downfall.

Peaches blush, wear silly hats,
While cherries giggle as they chat.
The sun shines bright, a golden grin,
As fruit bats playfully swoop in.

Now gather 'round, take a chance,
Join the harvest's silly dance.
With laughter sweet as honeyed tea,
Nature's joke is plain to see.

Gemstones in the Grove

In the grove where laughter's found,
Fruits are jewels upon the ground.
With ruby red and emerald green,
They giggle in sun's glowing sheen.

Oranges toss like playful balls,
While plums wear purple, making calls.
A grapevine swings, what a display,
As fruits chat lively, come what may.

Bananas slip in a slip-and-slide,
While pomegranates boast with pride.
Lemons grin with a sour note,
Telling jokes, not one remote.

So grab a snack, don't take it grave,
In this grove, we all misbehave.
With nature's wealth, we laugh and cheer,
For gemstones are fruit, oh dear, oh dear!

Fruits of Labor's Love

Workers toil with smiles so wide,
As berries bloom, they burst with pride.
A farmer trips, oh what a sight,
His pitchfork dances, oh what a flight!

Mangoes roll like bowling pins,
As laughter drowns the sun's sweet sins.
The corn stalks gossip tall and bright,
While carrots jest, oh what a sight!

Apples bob in a festive tub,
The pumpkins giggle, form a club.
Ripe strawberries sing in the breeze,
While rhubarb cracks jokes with such ease.

Together we harvest, share the cheer,
With every chuckle, we'll persevere.
In labor's grasp, we find the glow,
As fruits of love in antics grow!

Liquid Sunshine in a Jar

Jars line up, all bright and merry,
Filled with treasures, sweet and cherry.
Tomatoes blushing, ready to pop,
While pickles dance from the very top.

Jam's a riot with berries in style,
A spoonful brings a silly smile.
Spilling laughter as peaches collide,
While the apricots take a ride.

Cucumbers giggle, so fresh and cool,
In briny waters, they play the fool.
Lemonade bubbles, what a delight,
Refreshing giggles in every bite.

So twist the lid, and pour a cheer,
Liquid sunshine, oh so dear.
With every sip, let flavors swirl,
Join the fun in a fruity whirl!

Banquet of Flora and Fauna

In the glade where critters feast,
Squirrels dance and rabbits tease.
Mice swing from the apple trees,
While bees buzz the latest breeze.

A raccoon dressed in a suit,
Counts his berries, what a loot!
While owls hoot and giggle too,
Sharing tales of morning dew.

The cherries burst with joyous cheer,
Each one, a clown, full of beer!
The hedgehogs roll in soft grass beds,
Telling jokes while flipping spreads.

At this party, all can join,
Even ants dance, oh what a coin!
With laughter soaring into the sun,
Nature's banquet—oh what fun!

Gatherings of Nature's Wealth

Gather round the leafy throne,
Where mushrooms wear a shiny cone.
Parrots squawk with cheeky glee,
As nature's wealth spills from the tree.

Grapes get tangled in a vine,
Wearing hats and sipping wine.
Turtles slow-dance on the ground,
While the butterflies spin round and round.

A playful raccoon, sly and spry,
Pretends he's an acrobat in the sky.
He jumps and flips to steal a pear,
Then laughs to watch the watchers stare.

With every crunch and merry shout,
Even the crickets laugh out loud!
They chirp a tune, a silly jest,
In gatherings where all are blessed.

Whimsy of Fruits and Flora

Oh, the fruits play hide and seek,
In colorful hats, quite unique!
Lemons laugh as they roll away,
While oranges start a dance ballet.

The flowers gossip with delight,
Making up tales, quite a sight.
Sunflowers wear sunglasses, bold,
As daisies tell secrets of old.

Strawberries giggle and tease the pine,
"Your prickles can't stop this vine!"
Pineapples nod, enjoying their fame,
At this party, we're all the same.

Laughter under a sky so blue,
Every bloom a friend so true.
Nature's whimsy, oh what fun!
Join the feast; it's just begun!

Embraces in the Garden of Abundance

In the garden, where laughter grows,
Tomatoes blush and corn all glows.
Zucchini roll with glee and play,
As peas chatter through the day.

The carrots wear their pointy hats,
As radishes boast of their stats.
They tell tales of mud pies made,
While turning each other's shade.

A butterfly flutters, imitating a dance,
While ladybugs give it a chance.
Together they twirl in the sunny gleam,
Creating a wholesome veggie dream.

So come join all, it's quite sublime,
In this garden, we laugh and rhyme.
With hugs and smiles from every sprout,
Abundance shines with joyful shout!

Celebrating the Gifts of Growth

In the garden where we sow,
Tomatoes roll, and peppers glow.
The carrots hide beneath the dirt,
While radishes plot to do some work.

Cucumbers wear a prickly grin,
While lettuce laughs, it's quite a win.
Zucchini's stretching like it's on a spree,
And all the veggies dance with glee.

A squash parade, all lined in green,
The best vegetables you've ever seen.
Spinach shows off in leafy attire,
While beets blush, but still aspire.

With baskets full, we share a meal,
A feast of fun, it's quite the deal.
With every bite, we shout hooray,
For growth has made our funny day.

Serendipity Among the Fruiting Rows

In rows so ripe, the fruits collide,
With apples brawling, they take a ride.
Peaches tumble in a fuzzy spree,
While cherries conspire, plotting with glee.

Bananas slip, a daring prank,
As melons giggle in the tank.
Grapes are hanging, oh what a sight,
Juggling juice in a fruit-filled fight.

Pineapples wear their spiky hats,
While plums argue about the stats.
With every splash, a fruit parade,
Nature's quirks, all in the shade.

As laughter echoes through the trees,
The fruits unite, perfect harmony.
For in this patch, joy's the goal,
Serendipity fills the bowl.

Palette of Nature's Exuberance

The garden glows in vibrant hues,
A rainbow riot, it's good news!
Radishes red, peppers yellow,
Each color bursts, a merry fellow.

Green beans dance upon their stalks,
While broccoli strikes silly talks.
Carrots wear coats of orange bright,
Competing in this lively sight.

Potatoes play hide-and-seek well,
Under the ground, they wish to tell.
Corn whispers secrets to the breeze,
While pumpkins bicker, if you please!

A palette made by nature's hand,
Where silly veggies joyfully stand.
With every meal, we toast and cheer,
For growth and laughter throughout the year.

Harvesting Echoes of Sunlit Dreams

In fields where sunlight sparkles bright,
Tomatoes blush in sheer delight.
With wobbly squash in a merry break,
Each fruit laughs, oh make no mistake!

Ripe strawberries hide under leaves,
While giggling peas plot their thieves.
And berries whisper sweet, sweet tales,
In the cool shade where laughter prevails.

Crisp apples roll, and side by side,
Join the chorus in this fruity ride.
The sun-drenched whispers, oh so keen,
Harvest time's a joyful scene!

As we gather and share our signs,
The echoes linger through the vines.
In every bite, the sweetness beams,
Harvesting echoes of sunlit dreams.

Seasons of Growth and Giving

In springtime's dance, the blossoms sway,
Bees buzzing loudly, come what may.
Fruit flies take flight with grand parade,
While gardeners blush, their plans delayed.

Summer rolls in with sun's hot glare,
Watermelons laugh without a care.
Cherries and peaches try to compete,
But all end up mashed, what a treat!

Fall brings the harvest, a jumbled mess,
Pumpkins roll by, I must confess.
Cider spills over like gossiping friends,
Who knew produce could cause amends?

Winter's left over, a frosty chill,
Canned fruits now watch us from the sill.
As we sip cocoa, dream of the sun,
And hope next year we'll have more fun!

Lush Canopies of Color

Under leafy greens, the chatter grows,
Squirrels plot mischief, as everyone knows.
Apples hang low, they hide from the sun,
While pears roll their eyes, saying, 'Join the fun!'

Peach trees gossip, their branches all sway,
'Who's been stealing our sun's warm ray?'
The plums throw a party, an unripe affair,
But grapevine's the DJ, spinning without care.

As colors blend in this fruity hall,
Bananas put on their best yellow shawl.
With laughter and juice, the breeze lightly tickles,
It's a rowdy bash, full of fruity giggles!

So come take a seat under color's embrace,
Join in the fun, don't leave out your grace.
In this canopy bright, we celebrate cheer,
With a wink from the trees, and maybe a beer!

A Feast for the Eyes and Soul

On the counter, a feast like no other,
Fruits piled high, just ask your mother.
A pineapple sports a quirky hat,
While kiwis whisper, 'What's up with that?'

Strawberries pose, standing tall and bright,
No one's told them it's nearly night.
The oranges roll, in the fruit bowl they dive,
While grapes climb high, feeling so alive.

Figs flip-flop, with no sense of fear,
'Life's just sweeter when friends are near!'
With laughter and jokes, the flavors unite,
As fruits serve themselves, what a sight!

So gather around, don't be shy, my friend,
This feast is a joy, and it will not end.
With colors and laughter, we'll savor the cheer,
A bounty of happiness, let's raise a beer!

The Nature of Giving

Give to the bowl, a wild fruity spree,
Each piece of nature, a gift from the tree.
Bananas exchange in a slippery way,
Daring each other, 'Who'll save the day?'

Lemons squeeze in with a zesty grin,
'Life's a bit sour, let the fun begin!'
While avocados declare, 'We've got the cream!'
A guacamole party? Now that's the dream!

Coconut laughs, with a shell so tough,
'You think I'm boring? You've no idea, snuff!'
As fruits trade secrets, their stories unfold,
The nature of giving, a sight to behold.

So take a big bite, and share with delight,
For laughter and love make everything right.
In gardens we thrive, we're never alone,
With fruity companions, we've each found a home!

Orchard Reflections in Golden Light

Amidst the trees so wide and grand,
A squirrel danced, unplanned and tanned.
He focused hard on his next big feat,
Dropping nuts—now that's a treat!

The apples giggled with a shiny grin,
While pears debated who's best to win.
In shadows cast by gleeful blooms,
The bees built homes with little rooms.

A farmer slipped on fallen fruit,
And rolled like an acrobat, so cute.
The crows just cawed, they knew the score,
This show was free—who could ask for more?

With laughter echoing through the air,
Nature's antics sparked the flair.
A pie was born from a silly blunder,
As friends gathered for the all-too-funny plunder.

Soulful Harvests of the Land

The corn stalks whispered secrets prime,
While pumpkins plotted a prank at prime time.
They claimed the squash should wear a hat,
But mischief fell flat—imagine that!

Tomatoes blushed in hues so bright,
As rabbits danced under the moonlight.
Each veggie dreamt of tasty delight,
While yet another critter took flight.

With baskets full of veggie cheer,
The harvest folks held their laughter dear.
A goat joined in, made a grand old mess,
Leaving greens in a very funny dress.

To share the bounties that they find,
They coupled their goodies with jokes combined.
With laughter ringing clear as bells,
Who knew that farming could bring such yells!

Nature's Treasure Trove Uncovered

Beneath the sunlit branches wide,
A raccoon took his nightly ride.
He stumbled on a stash of treats,
With chips and dips—oh, nature's feats!

The walnuts laughed and rolled with glee,
As acorns planned a little spree.
Dancing around, they turned quite spry,
Who knew that woodlands could get so high?

A butterfly fluttered in swoops of blue,
While mushrooms peeked through morning dew.
With an earthworm's wormy mumble,
They held a concert—a squishy jumble!

At dusk, nature's jokes took flight,
Every critter joined in the delight.
In this treasure trove of giggles loud,
Who knew plants could form such a crowd?

Clusters of Joy in the Boughs

In branches high where laughter swings,
Chirping birds began their flings.
One dove headfirst, just for fun,
And rolled into a pile—oh what a run!

Grapes intertwined in a grapey jest,
While oranges aimed for a fruity fest.
The lemons sighed, too sour to play,
As berries bounced in a cheerful array.

With peaches perched on the highest tier,
They tossed down giggles, both loud and clear.
Each splash of juice was a playful cheer,
Nature's jokes spread far and near!

From leafy nests to sunlit floors,
Their laughter echoed through the doors.
Clusters of joy in the branches abound,
Who knew such fun could always be found?

Cradle of Seasons and Cycles

In springtime, squirrels play sneak,
Chasing apples, they find a peak.
With bloated cheeks, they dive and roll,
Harvesting snacks that fill their hole.

Summer sun makes the fruit all swell,
Juicy berries under a spell.
A plump peach stole my picnic chair,
I swear it winked, and I swear it dared.

In autumn, pumpkins sing their tune,
They dance in patches beneath the moon.
Ghosts of veggies trying to fright,
Beware the squash with a sense of fright!

Winter wraps its cold, frosty hand,
As squirrels team up to make a band.
With nutty jokes that tickle the frost,
In the cycle of seasons, laughter's never lost.

Tides of Nature's Richness

The trees gossip with a playful grin,
Telling secrets of where they've been.
While tomato vines throw shade at corn,
"Who's got more style?" they boast and scorn.

Beneath bright leaves, ants waltz along,
Carrying crumbs, they form a throng.
But tiptoe softly! Watch your shoes,
You might just squash their latest muse!

Cucumbers compete in the humor race,
They laugh at each other, a veggie embrace.
With whispers of pickles in their dreams,
They scheme their takeover in saucy themes.

As the seasons dance in a wacky twist,
Nature concocts a fun-filled list.
With laughter sprouting from earth's rich bed,
Tides of joy in the garden spread!

Gathering Dreams from the Greenhouse

In a greenhouse where the daisies play,
Tomatoes plot their daring getaway.
With giggles sprouting from leafy beds,
"We're ripe for mischief," the parsley said.

Carrots whisper, "You won't believe,
The radishes wear the crowns we weave."
As bees buzz by with a dance so grand,
They're drawing plans just to take a stand.

Cucumbers jest, "We stand tall and bright,
While you're just roots—out of sight!"
But each seed knows in their green little hearts,
There's magic in growth, and it's all about arts!

As sunlight beams and laughter rolls,
Every plant here has lofty goals.
Gathering dreams, both silly and sweet,
In the greenhouse, where the world's a treat.

Ephemeral Beauty in the Grove

In the grove, cherries wear party hats,
While squirrels have dance moves that go splat!
A peach slips by, waving its fuzz,
Shouting, "Catch me if you can! Just because!"

The daisies twirl in their frock of white,
Their petals whisper, "We'll dance all night!"
But watch the bees—those little jesters,
They buzz around like uninvited investors.

Grapes hang low, with a smile so round,
Hosting their friends in the viney ground.
But when it rains, they squeal with glee,
"Splash upon us, it's a jubilee!"

Fleeting joy in nature's embrace,
Every bloom wears a laugh on its face.
In this grove, the fun is never lost,
With ephemeral beauty, we count the cost!

Salutations to Burgeoning Blooms

Oh flowers, with your colorful hats,
You dance in the breeze, like acrobatic bats.
Saying 'hello' in shades so bold,
Who knew a flower could also be gold?

The bees applaud as they buzz around,
Spreading joy with every sound.
But watch your step, dear clumsy friend,
For pollen's a prankster, and it does not end!

Sweet Secrets of Fruition

In the garden, fruits giggle and sway,
Telling tales in a sugary way.
A berry whispers to its tart kin,
'Why do we wear ruby coats to begin?'

A banana slips, with a comedic frown,
Saying, 'I'm appealing, don't throw me down!'
The apples just chuckle, wise and round,
In this fruity circus, laughter's abound!

Harmony in Nature's Lush Palette

In shades of green, the leaves start to croon,
While flowers burst forth, like a joyful tune.
The daisies debate on who's fluffiest here,
While the tulips gossip, their voices all cheer.

A butterfly flutters, spreading wild cheer,
Saying, 'In this chaos, there's nothing to fear!'
The shrubs are just happy, with roots all a-sway,
Living life leafy, come join the play!

Colors of Delight After Rain

The droplets tumble, like laughter below,
Leaving giggles on leaves, with a sparkling glow.
A puddle forms, a mirror to the sky,
Reflecting the antics, oh my, oh my!

The raindrops tickle the ground, what a show,
As worms wiggle up, with enthusiastic 'hello!'
And frogs join the choir, singing songs of the damp,
In this post-rain revelry, we all take a stamp!

Abundant Roots and Ripened Dreams

In a garden where tomfoolery grows,
Carrots dance in their leafy clothes.
Tomato kids play hide and seek,
While peas are giggling, oh so cheek!

Pumpkins plan a grand parade,
While radishes join in, unafraid.
With roots that tickle and shoots that gleam,
It's a plant-based riot, or so it seems!

Fruits juggling like a circus affair,
Playful melons rolling everywhere.
Bananas wearing hats so round,
This garden's a laughter-filled playground!

When the crops come forth, it's quite the sight,
With every veggie hoping for a bite.
So let's feast on this whimsical scheme,
Where roots dig deep, and dreams redeem!

Sweetness in the Air

In the orchard where giggles collide,
A bee with a bowtie takes a ride.
Lemonade trees shake in delight,
While cherries throw a party at night.

The pears wear glasses, quite dapper indeed,
While oranges plot a daring speed.
"Let's race to the sun!" they gleefully shout,
As limes giggle softly, getting about.

Hummingbirds hum a funny old tune,
While berries pickpocket under the moon.
"Sweetness is key!" they chant in a cheer,
As the pie crust's aroma draws everyone near.

With laughter around, the branches sway,
And the fruits play pranks in a fruity ballet.
A punchline of flavors, ripe for the snare,
In this blissful place, there's sweetness in the air!

Harvesting Hopes from Gnarled Trees

Beneath the gnarled trees with great big grins,
Wobbly apples play with their skins.
"Pick me! No me!" they shriek with glee,
While squirrels join in the dizzy spree.

Pomegranates burst into giggles aloud,
Laughing at berries, so colorful and proud.
"Let's make a juice that tickles the tongue!"
As figs swing low, getting all the fun!

Amidst the branches, a raccoon will slide,
Stealing some peaches with fibs as his guide.
"Don't tell the others!" he winks and he grins,
While mulberries roll, avoiding the spins.

With a harvest of hopes, all wild and free,
Each fruit tells a tale of pure jubilee.
So here in the trees, with laughter and play,
We gather the joys of a bright, fruitful day!

A Tapestry of Sunlit Delights

In the sunlight, surprises abound,
Where strawberries hide in the ground.
"Can you find me?" they giggle with glee,
As bees wear sunglasses humming with spree.

Peaches converse with the summer breeze,
"Pass the lemonade, if you please!"
While grapes craft a shadowy line,
Swinging and swaying, feeling just fine.

A mango jester paints the air bright,
Pineapples dance, what a curious sight!
A chorus of fruits sings out from the tree,
Each one adding a note to the spree.

This tapestry weaves joy without end,
Where every fruit is a cheerful friend.
Under the sun, with laughter ignites,
A harvest of giggles and sunlit delights!

Ripened Joys on Sunlit Paths

In the sunny glade, the fruits all prance,
Plums in pajamas, they dare you to dance.
Cherries chuckle and apples grin wide,
While the pears throw a party, oh what a ride!

Grapes wear their vines like crowns on their head,
While figs tell stories, they've got quite a spread.
Peaches get cozy, all dressed up in fuzz,
Bananas in bonnets, oh what a buzz!

Lemons are lemons, they still crack a joke,
Oranges play pranks, they're the life of the smoke.
Berries in baskets behave like a clown,
Spreading their laughter all over the town!

Under the sunshine, where giggles abound,
The fruits are all feasting, oh, joy to be found!
With laughter and sweetness, they brighten the day,
In this fruit-filled fiesta, come join and play!

The Alchemy of Earth and Sky

In the garden of wonder, where tomatoes sit neat,
Carrots wear sunglasses, looking quite sweet.
Potatoes on tricycles, zooming around,
Make root vegetable races, with cheers all around!

The cucumbers giggle as they twist and they turn,
While radishes rally, it's their time to burn.
Herbs in a huddle are plotting a feat,
To turn this dull soil into a feast!

Strawberries wear hats made of leaves and some strings,
They dance on the grass as the morning bird sings.
Peas in their pods have a pun-derful tale,
Of how simple veggies can never go stale!

Beneath the blue skies, the laughter cascades,
With greens and with roots in a merry charade.
The earth brings a smile, the sky paints it bright,
In this garden so silly, all's perfectly right!

Fables from the Land of Trees

In the canopy high, where the squirrels debate,
Oaks tell tall tales that keep them up late.
Maples weave legends of syrupy cheer,
While willows roll laughter, making all appear clear!

Bamboo's got rhythm, it dances with grace,
Palm trees are models, it's a fashion showcase.
Spruce tells a secret, a conifer's dream,
Of pine-scented adventures that brighten the theme!

The fruit trees gossip, comparing their yields,
Peach trees tease apples about their soft shields.
Orchards evolve into comedy nights,
With branches all shaking, sharing giggly sights!

Yet under the stars, in a rustling tune,
Nature's own choir sings out to the moon.
With laughter entwined in the roots of the land,
Forever they thrive, a funny little band!

Crisp Days and Juicy Nights

As autumn arrives, with its crispy delight,
Pumpkins wear smiles on a cool moonlit night.
Cider's on tap, with a sparkle and fizz,
The apples can't help but dance with a whizz!

In sweaters of flannel, the fruits take their place,
Bobbing for goodies, it's a juicy embrace.
Crisp, crunchy leaves make a playful old sound,
While figs in their jackets are all gathered 'round!

Grapefruits recite poems with zest in their voice,
While pears play charades, oh, isn't it choice?
Together they mingle, all cozy and bright,
On this whimsical eve, under soft-stringed light!

So here's to the flavors, the giggles, the fun,
With laughter and sweetness, let the harvest run.
In a world of delight, where the fruits take their flight,
Crisp days and juicy nights, what a truly grand sight!

www.ingramcontent.com/pod-product-compliance
Lightning Source LLC
Chambersburg PA
CBHW070317120526
44590CB00017B/2721